D0682986

QUESTIONS

By the same author
THE WAY I SEE IT

QUESTIONS

by

CLIFF RICHARD

HODDER AND STOUGHTON

Copyright © 1970 by Cliff Richard
First printed 1970

SBN 340 10545 3

All rights reserved. No part of this publication may
be reproduced or transmitted in any form or by any
means, electronic or mechanical, including photo-
copy, recording, or any information storage and
retrieval system, without permission in writing from
the publisher.

This book is sold subject to the condition that it
shall not, by way of trade or otherwise, be lent,
re-sold, hired out or otherwise circulated without
the publisher's prior consent in any form of binding
or cover other than that in which this is published
and without a similar condition including this condition being imposed on the subsequent purchaser.

Printed in Great Britain for Hodder and Stoughton
Limited, St. Paul's House, Warwick Lane, London,
E.C.4. by Cox & Wyman Limited, London, Reading
and Fakenham.

CONTENTS

ILLUSTRATIONS

Between pages 48 and 49

ACKNOWLEDGEMENTS

1 Clifford Shirley   2 Eastern Daily Press
3 Dezo Hoffmann Ltd.

QUESTIONS
Lyrics copyright, published by
permission of Joaneline Music Ltd.

How to start . . . What to say?
I can't remember ever feeling this way.
Can it be true?
Does anybody care?
Is it only make-believe, or are you really there?

Is there a chance I've been missing the best?
Could it be life is more than a guess?
I'm afraid to let go,
Yet I long to see—
If you are real, be real to me.

O.K., supposing I
Were to come to you—
Not saying I will,
But just supposing I do:
Would I have to be
Just another guy?
Two a penny's not for me,
It just won't satisfy.

QUESTIONS

I'm just confused by candles and prayers.
I just need to know if you are there.
Show me the way, for I long to see—
If you are real, Lord, be real to me.

James F. Collier and Cliff Richard

Introduction

The world is full of questions, and not too many answers. That's what I've discovered in the last few years.

When I wrote *The Way I See It*, I thought I'd answered once and for all most of the questions I was ever likely to be asked. But a year or two have passed since then, and still the questions come thick and fast. Every time I go to speak at a student or school meeting, or sing at a youth club, or even have a few friends round on a Saturday night, I find myself pinned in a corner being questioned.

It's probably all my own fault. Ever since I began my career I've tried to give answers to questions people ask. The answers have changed over the years, but I suppose it's got around that I'm one of those people who's prepared to stick his stupid neck out when requested.

I remember going to a party in a friend's flat. It was noisy and crowded—most of the people there were in show-biz, one way or another. I squeezed into a room, and literally before I could even get to a wall to lean on I was cornered.

"This religion bit—is it for real?"

"How can you be so sure you're right?"

"It's a good P.R. line, isn't it?"

When I managed to get away about two hours later I'd done absolutely nothing at the party except try to answer questions about Christianity and my own part in it. I don't think anybody was exactly converted, but at least I'd been able to clear up a few very common misunderstandings.

Now I'm not an expert on religion, and I'm not a writer, either. But I feel there's a bit of a duty involved when so many people are asking so many questions—and many of the questions they ask are about really important things. Perhaps because they feel they 'know' me, questions which really ought to go to parsons and theologians somehow land on my plate. At any rate, I felt one possible way to deal with them was to try to write another book based entirely on things people have asked me, and which I have not answered in print before.

Cliff Richard is not infallible! My opinions are no more valid than yours. But what I've tried to do with the 'important' questions is to find out what the Bible says—and, for me, that's like saying, what God says—and then to apply it to the problem. You can do what you like with my opinions, but when God has spoken about something ... well, that's rather different, isn't it?

I don't believe in ramming my religion down other people's throats, and I don't want to set myself up as a moral guide to mixed-up fans. But people who ask me things are entitled to an answer—and that's why I've called this book *Questions*. They're your questions, and my answers—not very brilliant, but honest, I hope, and straightforward. Like *The Way I See It* they cover all sorts of subjects, from the frivolous to the profound, from my views on mini-skirts to what I believe about the Holy Spirit. It's rather a weird mixture, but I hope you enjoy it.

Happiness

Would you say you were a happy person? Happier now than a few years ago? Does the fact that many other people in the world are unhappy or suffering rob you of your happiness? What sort of things upset, annoy or distress you? Could you be happy and poor? Or on your own? Or unsuccessful? Would you be as happy if you left show-biz? Do you actually enjoy all these religious meetings you go to?

Basically, I suppose I am a happy person. At least, I'm not very often miserable or depressed, and I certainly enjoy life. Let me quickly say, I was happy long before I was 'famous'. We had some wonderful times as kids, although we were never well off—and for a long time we were very poor. We arrived in England from India with exactly five pounds, and squeezed in with a grandmother who had eight children in the home. For seven months after that dad was unemployed, and later on we lived six people to a single room. Yet we were a very happy family, and I can remember more happy and enjoyable times than the other sort.

So I don't think money, as such, has got a lot to do with it. I know plenty of people who are rich and miserable—in fact, many really wealthy people are basically discontented. Happiness is in your thinking, your attitudes, more than in circumstances.

Of course I've enjoyed being successful, and my career has brought me a lot of pleasure. I've seen the world, and been able to enjoy many of the luxuries that other people can't afford. But I've often said—and I hereby say it once again—that I know I can be happy without being rich, and I'm sure I could be perfectly contented on, say, a school teacher's salary.

After all, one of the biggest factors in happiness is our relationship with other people. I suppose more people commit suicide over 'relationships' than anything else. No-one can be completely happy on his own. I honestly believe now that the relationships I value most have nothing to do with my being rich or famous, and I don't think I'd lose any friends worth losing if my next record never made the top nine hundred and I wasn't heard of again.

What it really amounts to is that since I became a Christian I've got a better perspective on this happiness business. If happiness depends on relationships, then I know now that it depends most of all on our relationship to the Person who made us, God Himself. If our relationship with Him is all right, then we are well on the way to true happiness. If it's wrong, then no matter how rich, successful or popular we may be, we shall never achieve true happiness.

That's why I'm happier now. I think I've grown up a lot since I became a Christian. I know myself better and I'm not so easily swayed by things that seem important at the time, but really don't matter very much at all. I know that God has accepted me, through His Son Jesus Christ, and that matters to me much more than what other people think of me or say about me. That gives you a better sense of priorities and puts criticism and praise into their right place.

Unhappiness usually comes from being let down, or from failure or disappointment. Obviously these still have power to hurt me, but I think they would affect me much less now—and much less permanently— than they would have done a few years ago. God never lets anyone down, and he is never a disappointment.

This unhappy world

Sometimes, when I've been talking like this, someone has chipped in and accused me of not caring much about all the suffering in the world. How can you be happy and contented, they ask, when so many of your fellow human beings are starving, or being tortured, or bombed, or homeless? Hasn't Christianity blinded you to the sadness and misery of the world in which we live?

I think we need to be absolutely honest about this. When I see the Oxfam posters, or films of the people in Vietnam or Biafra, I feel all sorts of emotions— anger, frustration, a deep sympathy—but I couldn't really say they make me unhappy. I'll probably be criticised for saying this, but the fact remains that I can only be *unhappy* about things or people I am personally involved with. If the child of a friend was starving it would make me bitterly unhappy. But if the starving child is ten thousand miles away, in a village I've never even heard of, then it tends to isolate me from the problem emotionally. You can feel and share in other people's sorrow, but you can only feel it deeply if you know them.

For Biafra we can feel sympathy and frustration— nobody should have to suffer like that. At times I can feel distress and anger, too. But I'm not sure I could claim that that is 'unhappiness'. Perhaps part of the frustration we feel over suffering in general is just this —that we know it's there, and there's so little we can do—and we can't even feel it deeply, personally.

I realise that some—many young people, especially

—take a more idealistic view. They seem to argue that we should love everyone—every single person in need—with the sort of real, personal, individual love we have for our own wives or children, or as God has for us. I just can't see that this is possible.

How can you love someone you don't even know? God can love 'the world' because he alone is able to know every single one of us. If I, too, claim to love 'the world', I am also claiming to be God.

Let me spell this out. We are called to love everyone —in a general sense. We are to *care* about their conditions and their needs, even if we don't know them. But in its more restricted—and usual—sense, love involves knowing the person to be loved, understanding them and having a real relationship with them. Obviously I can't love 'Biafra' or 'Vietnam' in that way. Only God can love millions of people in a personal and equal way.

So, while I *do* care—if I may say so, more and more strongly—about suffering and need all over the world, I would be a hypocrite if I said it made me unhappy. And I reckon most other people would agree with me. Frustration, anger, even distress—these are my feelings in the face of human suffering. But I can't say that they often, and certainly not for long, rob me of my basic 'happiness'.

Things that get under the skin

In fact, foolishly, often much smaller things irritate more sharply. Quite a number of fairly small actions and attitudes upset or annoy me.

High on the list come people who criticise, or spread rumours, based on no personal evidence whatsoever. I've had quite a bit of this. I find it very irritating, and when I get these comments face to face I am tempted to hit back hard and below the belt. It usually isn't very hard to demolish people who go in for this sort of thing, because, having no real evidence or personal experience to back up their remarks, they can fairly easily be discredited.

I remember one acquaintance who gave out his views on Billy Graham ("It's all emotionalism, ends justifying means" and so on). Under questioning, he had to admit he'd never actually attended a Billy Graham meeting. Now *that*, to me, is pure emotionalism!

I also get quite a lot of criticism based on things I'm alleged to have said or done, but based only on rumour or hearsay. That is irritating, too—to say the least. Shows, records and songs are also sometimes dismissed by people—even professional critics—who don't bother to watch them or listen to them but simply say something like, "Oh I know what it will be like if *he's* doing it . . ." We've seen something of that in the reviews of *Two a Penny*, and in the attitude of some people to the *Life with Johnny* series—deciding in advance what it's going to be like and coming to it with prejudices at the ready.

An even smaller thing that upsets me—and I'm well aware it shouldn't—is when I fail to do something that I've put my hand to. For instance, I was asked to lead a discussion in our Crusader Bible class, and it was such a farce that I had to give up and just give them a talk instead. I reluctantly decided that I've still got a lot to learn about leading discussions. It upset me, I suppose, because I felt I'd fallen down on the job . . . something that was my responsibility. Probably it was really just annoyance at my own failure.

I'm also upset—again, probably more than I should be—by adverse criticism, professionally. This is particularly so when I feel that the critic hasn't been fair or made any effort to see what we were trying to do. The critics' treatment of *Two a Penny* really upset me, because I didn't feel they'd given the film a chance or really come to it with open minds. Still, I'm probably much too sensitive about this, and many performers and other public figures have had to put up with far more and uglier criticism than I have had.

But none of these things has cost me a night's sleep,

even. In fact, the only things that have caused me sleepless nights over the last few years have been a couple of family disagreements—which seems to prove the point that it is our closeness to people, rather than the nature of the trouble itself, that causes the distress.

Poor, but happy

Could I be poor and happy? That's a question I often get asked, and, as I've said already, I know that the answer is yes, because I have been poor and happy in the past. But it would probably be more difficult now that I have had the experience of comfort and luxury. However, almost everything I count really important has nothing to do with money, so I can't see why a change in financial circumstances should basically change my attitudes to life.

The question of quitting show-business is more complicated. In fact, it has practically nothing at all to do with being rich—or poor. I didn't go into show-biz in the first place for the money, and if I decided to give it up I don't believe money would influence my decision either way. The main issue here is simply one of obedience to God's will for my life. Not "Do I want to quit show-biz?", but "Does God want me to?"

Almost as soon as I was converted this question

arose. Not that others raised it, but just in my own thinking. Obviously the work a Christian does is a big factor in his life, and if all life comes under God's control it's reasonable to expect that He will control this part, too.

Now my first reaction was to pull out of show-biz and train to teach Religious Education. There were a number of reasons. For one thing, I was quickly aware of the pressures show-biz life puts on the Christian. It makes demands on your time that complicate your private life and cut you off from doing regular Christian work. It involves you in working alongside acts which you may feel are in bad taste or offensive. It puts you in a place where your beliefs are under pretty constant attack from people who entirely reject Christian standards. And so on.

So I told my manager and some of my friends that I wanted to phase out of show-biz and, provided I could pass the necessary number of G.C.E. subjects, go to a teacher training college at a date two or three years into the future. This was picked up by some of the papers and a private decision became public property.

However, in the meantime I'd had second thoughts. Some people have seemed to imply that once an opinion is reached it should never be changed, but that seems to me ridiculous. I'd by then had the chance

to talk this over with many more Christians, and I'd
had a year or two's experience of actually *being* a
Christian in show-business. I'd also gone some way to
re-arranging the way I worked so as to leave adequate
time for Christian worship and other activities.

Slowly I came to feel that if I quit show-biz it would
be like a rat leaving a sinking ship.

You see, I'd discovered, somewhat to my surprise,
that there were other active Christians in show-
business, in far more difficult circumstances (most of
them) than I was. My modest little stand for Christ
had obviously encouraged some of them a great deal
—just as their stand has encouraged me since then.
Should I pull out—with all my advantages as an
established performer, able to be pretty choosy about
his work—and leave them to get on with it? It was as
much some of these active Christians in the entertainment world as anything else that swayed me to stay
in and not quit.

The other big factor was the opening up of many
new ways of witnessing to Christ through my work.
Up till then I'd thought only in terms of speaking and
singing, in a limited way, at meetings and rallies. But
now I was invited to make a Christian film, my record
company wanted to release a Gospel album, there
were other opportunities on the horizon in television
and through much more effective and polished

personal 'performances'. Again, was all this to be passed up? My earlier decision began to look rather selfish, based more on my own comfort than on the guidance of God.

Surely, as a Christian living in a non-Christian world, I should expect pressure and learn to cope with it? This would be as true in a factory as on a film set. Running away from the world is no answer to its challenge ... so I decided to stay put. Paul told the Christians at Corinth to stay in the position in life they were in when they were converted.

I'm a professional entertainer. That's my job. As I see it now, my responsibility is to do that job to the best of my ability and to the glory of God, until He calls me to leave it and do something else. It does not seem to me any 'worldlier' than being a bank manager (handling filthy lucre) or shop-keeper. There is nothing specially immoral or sordid about the job itself, provided you don't allow yourself to be carried away by the glamour or the financial rewards. In fact, I find now that being in show-biz is good for me, because it tests what I believe and so strengthens my own faith.

I feel I have a duty to the little circle of active Christians in show-biz, and also to the much wider circle of people in the profession who are searching and questioning about God. Why should this 'trade',

alone of them all, be without Christian witness? Yet
if the Christians all pulled out, that would be the
situation—and, honestly, nobody from 'outside' has a
chance of making any real impact for Christ in this
terribly private world of show-biz. Since it became
known that I had decided, at any rate for the present,
to continue as an entertainer, I have had so many
opportunities to talk about Christ with show-biz
people—famous and not-so-famous—that I can't
doubt it was the right decision. Some have become
Christians. Others are still thinking it out. Others
have decided it's not for them—but at least they will
never be able to say that nobody ever told them what
Christianity is all about.

From my own personal point of view, I think I've
just about got the balance right at the moment. I have
Sundays free, and divide the rest of my time between
professional engagements and Christian work—visit-
ing schools, youth fellowships, hospitals and so on.

Now I realise that this is a very personal decision,
and I'm not saying that anyone else should necessarily
do what I've done. As far as I am concerned, I'm sure
it is right for me to be in show-biz, but I am quite prepared to believe that it would be equally right for
someone else to pull out of it and serve God in another
field altogether. There are no rules about these
decisions—except that there are no rules!

Don't let me give you the idea that I'm a reluctant performer, or that I don't enjoy my work. Of course I do—and all the more now that I can try to do it for God's glory and to please him. I get a great kick out of live performances, I like and get on well with most of the people I have to work with, and—like anybody else—I enjoy success.

All those meetings

But some people, who accept completely that I enjoy performing, find it hard to believe that I can possibly enjoy Christian meetings. Hymn-singing, prayers and sermons aren't their scene at all. But then they weren't mine, either, not so long ago.

Meetings vary, I must admit. Some are very much better organised and attended than others. But I do enjoy meeting Christians in towns up and down the country, and sharing experiences and difficulties with them. The Christian Church is a bit like a huge, open club. Anybody can join, and members recognise each other and get together whenever they can. It's an amazing thing to realise that pretty well anywhere you go in the world you've got friends.

Actually, though, you can have too much of a good thing, and there came a time when I seemed to be dashing from one meeting to another, with no time for any 'social' life and not much time for my own church, either.

My trouble is that I find it very hard to say 'no'. If people come up to me, or ring up, and ask if I'm free to speak to their youth group or school Christian union or something, and I know there's nothing in my diary, I often just can't bring myself to say that flat negative which is the only thing capable of deterring them completely. So I end up at their meeting, perhaps in between rehearsals or after a late night recording session the previous day, wondering for the millionth time how I let myself get talked into it. Yet, to tell the truth, I nearly always enjoy the meeting!

There are, I'm afraid, a few unscrupulous characters around, even in Christian circles, and I've been the victim of them once or twice. I mean the sort of person who puts out that Cliff Richard is going to sing at his rally or speak at his meeting, packs in the crowd, and then tells them I've let them down or cancelled at the last minute. In fact, so far I've never had to let anybody down at the last minute, even though at times it's meant chartering a car and chauffeur to shoot me across London from a television studio to a meeting. So if you come across some character claiming that I promised to come and then didn't turn up, check the facts before putting it round that I'm unreliable, would you?

The worst case of this, I think, was a man who announced in big newspaper ads. that I was to appear at his meetings in a certain town in the Midlands. In fact, I had all along said I couldn't appear, and he was well aware of that. Yet even when the meeting had begun he persisted in his story, telling the audience that my car had broken down on the M.1 but that I'd get there eventually. He even told them that he'd phoned my flat (I don't live in a flat, but—never mind!) and that he'd been assured I was on my way. Of course, the local papers claimed I'd let down the young people of that town, and I had to explain that I had never at any time given him the slightest reason to suspect that I was going to be at his meeting.

But these are, fortunately, rare exceptions. When it happens, mind you, it is a bit shattering, but I realise that there may be all sorts of twisted reasons why a person should act like that, and I remember all the kindness and friendliness that are usually shown me by ordinary Christian people who are doing a quiet, unspectacular job for God in a small youth club or in a factory or hospital or school.

They are the people who deserve all the help and encouragement we can give them—though, in a way, many of them are already the happiest people on earth.

I would be a Christian, but . . .

Church is boring and old-fashioned . . . I don't know how to believe . . . do I have to be 'converted'? . . . I tried, and failed—I couldn't keep it up.

I suppose the question I get asked most often of all by youngsters at school and youth meetings who are really interested in Christianity is, "Do you have to go to church to be a Christian?" They are attracted by the Christian message, but scared stiff of the church, which they think of as boring and old-fashioned. I must say, for three or four months after I became a Christian I refused to go to church—and in a way I'm glad I waited.

You see, you don't have to 'go' anywhere to be a Christian. I was definitely a Christian months before I started going to church. The dying thief crucified with Christ who was converted as he hung there alongside Jesus never got to church, but he was certainly promised heaven. But if you are a Christian, you will want to meet with other Christians to worship God.

If you've got the wrong approach to church—if you go to be entertained or thrilled—then you're going to end up by being bored, believe me. But my reason for going to church is very simply to join in worshipping God with other Christians, and with that attitude it just can't be boring. I really think the clue here is in ourselves and what we 'expect' from a church service—and are prepared to 'put into' it.

As for church being old-fashioned, there's no doubt in many ways it is. Some of the buildings are old, gloomy and draughty. Some of the language in the service (lots of it, in fact) is unlike any form of English spoken by present-day people. Very few of the hymn tunes were composed more recently than the Victorian era, and the new ones in most hymn books are very thin on melody—instantly forgettable.

But if church is important—and it's a brave man who says worshipping God doesn't matter—then don't stand outside grumbling ... come on in and help us put it right.

I'm sure our services and buildings could be brighter, more welcoming. We badly need modern hymns with singable tunes (not Gospel songs, for worship services). I'm convinced the prayer book services of the Church of England will have to be modernised in language, if there's going to be any church at all in thirty years time.

Recently I've got myself more involved in this battle for progress in our own church. Most of our evening congregation is young, but for years we've had to mumble our way through the chanting of the psalms. This was raised at the church's annual meeting, and it soon became obvious that all but three or four people there would like to see the chanting of psalms ended. But for the sake of those three or four it was not completely abolished—though there was an immediate and great improvement, and metrical psalms seem to have taken over from chanting.

At one church I visited, where the usual congregation of thirty had swollen for the evening to over a thousand, the church leaders over coffee in the vicarage afterwards really dug their toes in on the matter of concessions to young people who might start attending the church. "Why should we change?" they asked, "we're the regulars, week in and week out."

But that attitude is suicidal. Young people being what they are, and have always been, they will simply refuse to come in on those terms. Now if the older, supposedly more mature Christians are going to be as belligerent as that, digging their heels in and saying 'no more change', then we shall be the last generation of church-goers. I really believe that. I don't mean that Christianity will die out, but 'going to church' will. Some other way for Christians to associate together will be found. But someone's got to budge— either the youngsters outside (or just inside) or the elders; and it won't be the kids. The future really lies in the hands of those who lead the church, and some of them, I'm afraid, just don't see how urgent this all is.

Actually, I'm now a member of our parochial church council, duly elected on—I'm glad to say— the nomination of one of our more senior church members. So I suppose I'm one of the elders who's got to be ready for change. Personally, I welcome it. But, in case middle age brings a hardening of the arteries, I made a resolve after our last annual meeting, and that was that no matter how old I get, I shall remember that there are other people coming along, and that even if I don't like their ideas, the church's future is theirs—they've got to live with it—and for the sake of the future I must be flexible and under-standing. I just hope I can keep my vow!

But the fact is, many churches—including the one I belong to—are trying very hard to change things and worship God in a relevant, modern but reverent way. All sorts of things are going on—new style services, experiments in music and even the lay-out of church buildings. I'd say this is a time of terrific change in the church—it's a pity so many people are staying outside complaining nothing's being done, rather than coming on in and lending a hand to speed up the process. Of course, plenty of churches are still stuck in the nineteenth century—or even earlier, actually! But they're a dying race, and there's no reason why you should choose to join a stick-in-the-mud church rather than a go-ahead one—so long as the true Christian message is taught and believed there.

Belief—and Believing

Sometimes young people say to me, "Look—I've believed in God and Christ all my life, through Sunday school and my teens right up to now. I accept everything in the creed as true. But it doesn't really mean much to me, and I don't seem to have this confidence and assurance that other Christians obviously have. What's wrong?"

Now this is in fact a question about the meaning of the word 'believe'. Many other questions can also be traced back to a misunderstanding of what that word really means. You can 'believe in' facts (that two and two make four, and so on)—or that Julius Caesar came to England, or even that Jesus Christ was the Son of God on earth. All you are doing is assenting to the accuracy of certain statements. According to James—the brother of Jesus—the devils in hell 'believe in' God in that way: they have to admit he exists.

Anybody can believe in facts. It's stupid not to. But Christianity is a *commitment* to the facts about Jesus Christ and God, not just an acknowledgement that they're true.

This is where the whole business of 'conversion' comes in. There are stacks of people who mentally assent to the truth of Christianity (or admire Jesus Christ, or get a lot of help from going to church) who have never committed themselves to Christ. They have never 'turned'—that's what the word 'conversion' really means—from life without God to deliberate and personal faith in him.

This doesn't necessarily mean a sudden, instantaneous conversion. Mine wasn't.

But it does mean that at some point in time, having questioned and been on the verge of commitment perhaps for a long time, you realise that a moment of truth has come for you and you must commit yourself to what you have discovered.

Most people seem to think that that moment has to come in a big meeting, or in the minister's study, or perhaps as you kneel by your bed in very intense prayer. But from what I have heard of other people's experiences with God, I reckon it can come at any moment to a person who has been searching and questioning sincerely. It could hit you in a super-market, or while driving your car, or mowing the lawn . . . that the answer is right there, in Jesus Christ, and that you must do something about it, and you ask Christ to take over your life there and then.

It didn't work

From time to time I meet people who have done that —have committed themselves, so far as they know, to Christ—and yet, they say, it 'hasn't worked'. That usually means that they find there are sins and failures that they haven't been able to overcome, or that they don't seem to have the joy and confidence that others have. They then begin to doubt whether they are really Christians at all. Was it all a big illusion?

Now there's a basic misunderstanding here. Christianity doesn't claim to change every aspect of a personality overnight. When you become a Christian, you are still *you*, basically the same person, but under a new control; and that control, or guidance, works for long-term changes, not short-term shocks.

Let me put it like this.

When you cross the border from Switzerland into Italy the scenery doesn't suddenly become Italian— it's still alpine, in fact. It's only as you go further into Italy that slowly the snow gets left behind and the sun gets warmer and it becomes obvious that you're in a different country. The border represents the moment of decisive change from one nation into another. But only as you press on into the new country can you expect to discover just how different it really is.

It's very much the same with Christian commitment. There is a moment of decisive change, when we step from unbelief into faith (from 'darkness into light' is how the Bible describes it[1]). But only as we press on into the Christian experience can we expect to discover just how very different it is from our old life. But if you have sincerely turned from sin and put your trust in Jesus Christ then you *have* crossed the border and begun a new life.

But you don't step over the 'Christian' border into sinless perfection—and the fact that we're never going to reach perfection on earth may help us to accept that we are going to fail from time to time, and will go on failing until the day we die. In fact, a big difference between the Christian and the non-Christian is that the Christian is very conscious of failure, while the non-Christian often reckons he's getting on very well, and is quite blind to his failures. The truth is, that we can't keep up the Christian life without constant help and strength from God. If 'keeping it up' depended solely on our efforts, most of us wouldn't

[1] 1 Peter 2:9

last ten minutes. But fortunately it doesn't depend on us, but on God, who is able to make a wonderful job of even the most unpromising material.

In any case, it's wrong to concentrate on failure. Christianity is a positive, not a negative, thing. All the Christians in my own circle of acquaintances whom I knew before they were converted are much better and happier people as a result. And that's true whether they themselves recognise it or not.

How far is too far?

Are you bothered about being 'with it'? Do you worry about keeping up with fashion? How about mini-skirts? And fashions in morals? Trial marriages ... abortion ... divorce? In fact, how far is too far?

For several years now I've been given the 'Best Dressed Singer' award—actually it's the 'Best Dressed Boy', but you have to draw the line somewhere! This means many people think of me as a bit of a dandy, and they get a shock when they find me lounging around in old jeans or a faded but favourite old shirt.

I must admit I like clothes, and I enjoy looking and feeling smart. I bet a lot of other men do, too, who would hotly deny it if asked. Fortunately, in the last few years it has stopped being considered a bit kinky for a man to choose to wear colourful or distinctive clothes. At one time I had more enthusiasm than taste where clothes were concerned (my black shirt and pink tuxedo period), but at least I can say I always felt that how you looked on stage was almost as important as how you performed.

That was one distinctive thing about the Shads—they always looked great, not only what they wore but the way the whole act was presented—movements, positioning, lights and so on. No-one—but *no-one*—has ever equalled them for that in the pop field.

I like to choose my clothes carefully. There was a time when I spent more money than I needed to on clothes, but now I like to feel I'm getting value for money. I seldom buy things like shirts, ties, socks and trousers in the West End these days—this isn't really for economy reasons, but simply that it seems wrong to pay more for things than you need to, or than they are worth in real terms.

I think that's where the whole question of fashion arises. For me, doing the job I'm doing, dressing carefully and well is part of my work. I don't think people should be asked to pay good money to watch a performer who can't even be bothered about his appearance. 'Off duty' I dress mainly to please myself —usually fairly casually, unless it's a special occasion. But still I feel that a certain standard is expected of those of us who earn our living by being public figures, and I wouldn't like to think people felt let down on meeting me!

But at the same time it's stupid and wrong to be a

slave to fashion. And even worse to try and get ahead of it. For a Christian this is a special problem—let me explain why.

Paul told the Christians at Rome two thousand years ago not to let the world around them "squeeze them into its own mould"[1]. We are not to be moulded and shaped by what everybody else does, but by what God wants. Obviously to get obsessed with keeping up with every whim of fashion is to let part of our lives be moulded and shaped by what others are doing, and so is wrong.

On the other hand, Jesus warned his followers that they weren't to make themselves look different from everybody else by deliberately refusing to follow the ordinary standards of dress or cosmetics. He told them[2] to put oil on their heads like everybody else (that seems to have been like a hair cream!), so that the difference between them and others wouldn't be their appearance, but their hearts.

Now if a Christian girl today goes around in long skirts, or a young Christian man wears baggy trousers or a long, trench-style raincoat, they are surely going against what Jesus said, and drawing attention to themselves by their outward appearance.

So it would seem that the proper balance is to keep

[1] Romans 12:2
[2] Matthew 6:16, 17

reasonably up to date with fashion, so that we don't look odd, but not worry about and not let the world dictate what we do and wear, especially if it's against our consciences.

Mini-skirts

Which brings me to mini-skirts. For some reason I can't quite understand, this subject seems to upset some older people almost more than anything else.

How mini is mini? I don't know. I should have thought this is a very personal thing for each girl to decide for herself. I can't really imagine that a few inches up or down makes all that difference to our nation's morals.

I suppose a mini is too mini when its length is not dictated by appearance (when the girl asks simply "Do I look better with it this length?") but by impact (when she asks "Will people notice me more if I have it even shorter?"). I have seen some grotesque sights in mini-skirts—you would almost think mirrors had never been invented.

Needless to say, mini-skirts have never been a personal concern of mine on stage! At least, not until a few people complained to me about the minis that Cindy sometimes wears on stage during our Gospel concerts.

Of course, that's nothing to do with me either—Cindy decides what she chooses to wear on stage. But I have said before (and gladly repeat) that you'd have to be either badly prejudiced or have a rather nasty mind to see anything immoral, sexy or harmful about her appearance in the concerts.

Mini-morals

Far more important than the trivial business of mini-skirts is the matter of mini-morals. Following the fashion in clothes may be harmful, but following blindly the fashion in behaviour or attitudes is moral suicide.

Here the pressure of the world around is much more subtle and terribly strong. 'Everybody does it' sounds a very convincing argument, but it isn't really.

Jesus said[3] that there are two roads through life, a narrow one leading to God, and a broad one leading to destruction. One is popular—"many go that way"—but it leads to disaster. The other is unpopular—"those who find it are few"—but it leads to life. Isn't it stupid to decide your route through life on the company rather than the destination? What's the point in having a great journey, with plenty of company, and then arriving at the wrong place? 'Everybody does it' may

[3] Matthew 7:13, 14

be true, as a statement of fact—but where does 'everybody' arrive? Fashion may help you choose between the right and wrong tie for a night out, but it will be a rotten guide to the right or wrong way to behave when the reefers are passed round, or pairing up for the night is suggested.

It's the same with all these modern moral questions —trial marriages (there's a stupid name for it, to start with—they're not 'marriages' at all), abortion, easy divorce and so on. If you believe there are standards, and especially if you believe, like me, that God set them, then it's the standards, and God himself, that matters, not what everybody else is doing. Many modern youngsters think they're being daring and unconventional and shocking, when in fact all they're doing is following the current fashion in their crowd like sheep—and bleating away about how 'free' they are. To me, that's the worst kind of slavery.

Serious readers, please omit

If you're in a hurry, or easily bored, or like to keep things in their right perspective, then please skip this chapter. It's full of trivialities from start to finish and I've only included it because if I'm supposed to be giving answers to questions I'm asked I have to admit that I do get asked these questions—and very frequently.

For some strange reason, the pop public is apparently fascinated by the minor details of the lives of the stars: what they like to eat and drink, their pets, their taste in socks, and so on. I say 'apparently', because this is what some papers and magazines give a lot of space to, and I don't suppose they would if their readers didn't enjoy it.

So, over the years, I've unburdened my heart about all these little things and they have been duly printed and publicised. The usual result is a flood of hand-knitted sweaters or green socks, if I've been so unwise as to say they are my 'ideal gift'.

The trouble is, I change my tastes pretty often, as most people do, and this leads to terrible confusion.

Also, I can't take many of these questions very seriously, but other people do—again, the results are confusing, to say the least. How can you answer the question, "What is your favourite drink?" My favourite drink, most of the time, is cold orange squash. But not last thing at night in mid-winter! Mostly, I suppose, I'd settle for milk. You see how difficult a simple question can be?

Anyway, here goes with answers to trivial questions, true as of this moment, but subject to change without notification in the future!

What are your vital statistics?

Even these vary! My height is (always) 5 ft. 10½ in. and my shoe size 7½. I used to weigh between eleven and twelve stone, but now usually keep my weight well below eleven most of the time. During the *Cinderella* run at the Palladium it even went below ten stone for a few days.

What are your favourite sports and games?

The only game I play seriously nowadays is bad-minton—I belong to the badminton club at my church and play pretty regularly through the winter. But I like almost all sports—soccer, tennis, swimming, whatever's going. I tend to be a competitive competitor. I like the rules to be observed, and I believe in playing to win.

Favourite food?

I've always liked curries (possibly that comes from my Indian background), but other than that what I like depends on where I am and what I'm doing. Usually I eat light meals, watching the calories, but every now and then I like to sit down to a real blow-out. When I do, I usually go for steaks, but it's the trimmings that really make the difference: especially well-cooked vegetables.

Odd things? Well, I sometimes drool over cauliflower cheese. I love steamed puddings, with the skin of the custard. And chip butties. If you don't know what they are, you haven't lived. I can enjoy lovely food, unusual tastes and exotic flavours. Or I can cheerfully settle for egg and chips.

May I add that a gastronomic highlight of the Crusaders' Broads cruises is my shepherd's pie. No substitutes—*real* shepherds.

What do you do about giving and getting presents? Isn't it a bit difficult for someone in your position?

Yes, it is. Obviously I get sent mountains of gifts and

presents from fans—sometimes they even throw them on to the stage. I was nearly concussed by a woolly monkey at the Palladium. But my friends know that I don't expect expensive presents. It really is 'the thought' that counts. And, so as not to embarrass people, I don't usually give presents outside my family and very close 'inner circle'.

Actually, I love giving presents and I also enjoy getting them—and their financial value is much less important to me than the thought and care that has gone into choosing them.

How do you relax?

Very well, actually! I can unwind quite quickly, and sleeping is no problem provided the room is really dark! But I suppose the question really refers to relaxing pastimes.

I enjoy driving, especially on long, open journeys. I've got a Jensen now, the best car I've ever had, and travelling in it is a pleasure and relaxation—out of town.

I think I could enjoy gardening, and do in moderation. We've got a medium-sized garden, but there's a lot of work to do in it that is routine and never-ending. Being away so much, I couldn't always do my share of the work, I'm afraid.

I can also relax over a meal, or in a good, lively conversation, or listening to music (other people's, usually).

Do you like pets? Have you got any?

We've got a budgie and a dog (Shandy). You can't get very emotional over a budgie (at least, I can't), but I'm quite attached to the dog, and I claim she obeys me better than anyone else.

What do you enjoy reading?

I don't read a lot of books, at least, not right through. Since I became a Christian, though, I've read more—in addition to the Bible, that is. Richard Wurmbrand's book *Tortured for Christ* impressed me tremendously.

I read a few magazines—*Crusade* (regularly), the *Church of England Newspaper* (sometimes), and the 'trade' press (when I have to).

What are your pet dislikes?

I could say, being asked, "What are your pet dislikes?"!

In general, I suppose, people who 'take liberties'. People who try to monopolise you. And people who try to use you for their own ends.

I don't like gossips, girls who chew gum, anybody who doesn't know when he's had enough to drink, loud voices, and too much make-up. And I don't like people who ask you questions and don't listen to the answer.

What do you find funny?

'Rowan and Martin's Laugh-In.'

I suppose my sense of humour is pretty normal. Like most people, I have to be in an hilarious mood really to split my sides, but it has been known to happen.

I don't like comics who have to resort to dirty jokes to get a laugh. I like even less comics who can be clean and very funny, but put in 'blue' material because they imagine it's what the audiences expect. I don't even think they're right, because many people are obviously embarrassed by it.

Have you met any of the Royal Family?

I was waiting for you to ask that!

Actually, I've been 'presented' at Royal Command performances, and so on, and I met Princess Margaret several years ago at a youth club she visited in Hackney, where the Shads and I had been invited to perform. She was very charming and, although I had

Thousands of faces! This is pretty typical of some of the Christian youth rallies I go to, in fact. This one was at Manchester, and there is Cindy with me, whacking the tambourine.

One man went to mow. Me. Still, it's an electric power mower, so there's no excuse for that agonised expression.

Captain at the wheel—of my cruiser *Pomander*.
On a Broads cruise with the Crusaders.

Safety first! Mind you, they still manage to fall in.

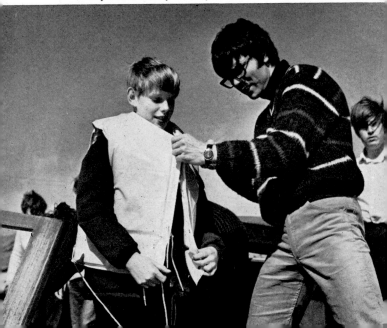

Great composers at work. Mike and John of the Settlers with yours truly at an arranging session. Don't know what the gents on the wall thought of it!

During a Gospel song concert. I particularly like this shot—taken during our performance in The Hague, Holland.

One of the greatest moments—with the Settlers at a mission service in Coventry Cathedral. The Bishop's there in the front row.

I'm not exactly Segovia, you know. As you can see, sometimes it's quite
hard work.

The Royal Albert Hall, and another big moment. I think the song was 'Glory, Glory, Hallelujah', and the young lady, of course, is Cindy Kent

laryngitis at the time and could only croak through the songs, we sat and talked at a tea party afterwards.

But the big event was an invitation to lunch with the Queen at Buckingham Palace. That was early in 1969. The Duke of Edinburgh and Princess Anne were there, too, and I must say (without going in for royal revelations) that it was very informal, friendly and enjoyable. The Queen is marvellous at making everybody feel easy and relaxed, and they all seem sincerely interested in their guests.

How do you choose the records you record?

I suppose that means how do we choose the songs? Like most singers, I get sent literally hundreds of 'demo discs' of new songs which their composers or publishers think might appeal to me. We listen to them, and if any seem possibles I play them over several times, trying to judge their appeal. Not every song I like is really suitable for me to sing and record, especially as a single.

I keep mentioning 'we'. The reason is that I don't make this sort of decision on my own. My manager, Peter Gormley, and my recording manager, Norrie Paramor, play a big part in the decision, though they would never try to persuade me to record a song that I didn't like.

Once we have decided that the song is worth recording, an arranger gets to work on it, and eventually I go along to the studios and record it, usually with a number of other songs. That still doesn't mean it will ever be on sale to the public! I record dozens of tracks, of which some end up on albums and a few—very few, naturally—as 'singles'. At any moment there is quite a supply of Cliff Richard material on tape—I prefer to work that way. In fact, very rarely have I gone into the studio knowing that I was going to record my next single—that decision is made after the number is recorded.

I'm not a believer, because . . .

*Christians are hypocrites . . . There's no God anyway . . .
If there is, Jesus isn't his Son . . . The Bible's a load of
old myths . . . I went to Sunday school and all that, and
just grew out of it . . . Religion's for old women and kids
. . . I prefer Buddhism, astrology, spiritualism . . . And
how do you know Christianity is the 'true' religion? . . . I
don't want to miss out on the fun.*

"Look," he said to me, "you can keep your Christianity. There's this bloke up our road—a churchwarden or something—and he is the most revolting person I've ever met. If he's going to heaven, then put me down for hell any day."

It always seems to me this is all a bit too easy. So there's this man up the road who claims to be a Christian. You've got some idea of what the standards of Christianity are supposed to be, and then you judge the whole religion by this one man because he doesn't measure up to them.

There are at least two big mistakes here, it seems to

me. The first is that everybody who goes to church is a Christian. A Christian is someone who has put his trust in Jesus Christ and been given new life by God. That's an 'inside' thing, and only God can read people's inner motives and thoughts. You may find yourself rejecting Christianity on the grounds that a person who is not a true Christian at all doesn't behave like one! If this man is as revolting as he sounds, then very possibly he isn't a Christian—just strictly a churchwarden!

But of course it wouldn't disprove Christianity if he were a Christian. Christianity doesn't depend on any single person. If it were to be judged on my life, or that of anybody who professed Christianity, it would fail, because everybody fails.

Christianity is either true, or it's not true. It's truth has got to do with certain alleged facts—about God, about a man called Jesus Christ, about the Bible, and so on. Facts don't stop being facts just because a churchwarden up the road is a bit nauseating.

Much more important is this objection about God —"There's no God anyway". The Bible says, "Whoever would draw near to God must believe that He exists and that he rewards those who seek him."[1]

Now I must admit there's no formula for proving God exists. You can't say, "Two and two makes

[1] Hebrews 11:6

God." I've sat through plenty of arguments on this one, and all I've learnt is that nobody can *disprove* God, and nobody can prove He exists, either.

I'd like to link it with another objection to belief that I often get thrown at me—that Jesus Christ wasn't the Son of God. You see, when people come at me with this 'prove God exists' line, I usually start talking about Jesus Christ, who said, "He who has seen me has seen the Father." In other words, if we can prove that Jesus is the Son of God, then obviously God exists ... and though God is for most people a vague idea, Jesus is a person of history, who actually lived on this earth just under two thousand years ago. At least we've got some facts to examine where he's concerned.

What are those facts? Well, he certainly lived, and we've got plenty of evidence (most of it in the Bible, but quite a lot of other evidence, too) about his life. Most people who have read the Gospels—and you can't really discuss this question seriously if you haven't—come to admire Jesus and the things he said and did. I think I can honestly say that I've not yet met anybody who has read the Gospels and not admitted afterwards that Jesus impressed them enormously, and that basically they have reckoned him a good man—perhaps one of the best men who ever lived. But then you have to throw at them the below-

the-belt punch-line that this man they admire and
agree is good said that he was the Son of God. Unless
we are prepared to say that this good man was a liar,
we've got to face up to this claim. Everything he is
reported to have done on earth bears it out. For me,
it's easier to believe Jesus is the Son of God than to
disbelieve it.

But what do Christians mean when they call Jesus
'Son of God'? I remember one terrific discussion
about this at a meal after a day's TV recording. What
became clear then was that Christians must be very
careful about their use of words, or else we merely
confuse instead of helping people.

By 'Son', where Christ is concerned, we obviously
don't mean 'son' in the normal physical sense; but in
every other way, such as his nature, and that he shares
the life of God, and that there's a 'oneness' between
God the Father and Jesus that is more than simply
physical, 'Son' is much the best word to describe it.
When he was on earth, incidentally, I believe Jesus
Christ was God's Son in a literal way too, because the
Bible tells us that the Holy Spirit 'came upon' Mary
when she was still a virgin and that was how Jesus was
conceived[2]. It was as though God planted the seed in
her womb. So Jesus on earth was human and divine,
Son of God and Son of Man.

[2] Luke 1:35

The Bible a load of myths?

That brings us back to the Bible again. If you reckon it's just a load of myths, then you won't be very impressed when I quote it as an authority. So—why do I take the Bible so seriously?

Usually this sort of criticism comes from people who have never read the Bible, or tried to see the relevance of what it has to say, but from pure prejudice decide that it's a 'load of myths'. It's enough for them that Adam and Eve are in the Bible: that alone, they reckon, is grounds for chucking away the whole Book.

The only way anyone who feels like that about the Bible is going to change his mind is by getting to grips with the whole Book—to find out whether, on examination, it really is all 'myth' or not. I'm pretty sure that anyone who reads the whole thing with an open mind would never make such a sweeping state- ment about it again. Not all of the Bible is meant to be taken literally—that's the mistake sects like the Jehovah's Witnesses make—but it's not hard usually to decide where it is claiming to be history and where it is poetic or allegory or something.

Sometimes people ask me what would happen to my faith (and especially to my trust in the Bible) if it were proved—absolutely definitely—that Adam and

Eve, Cain and Abel, Noah and some of the others never existed.

My answer is always the same. It wouldn't really bother me at all, because the crunch of Christianity is Christ, not details of Old Testament history. Mind you, believing in Christ naturally leads me to believe the Old Testament, simply because He did: that is why all of the Bible is real and important to me—it was to him. So long as Christ is real, then the rest fits into place. The only thing that could smash Christianity completely would be 'proof' that Jesus Christ wasn't for real—and it's stupid to build a whole case against faith in him on the grounds that one day something might turn up to disprove it. It's about as likely as someone finding proof that Mars is made of cheese.

Rejecting Christianity on those grounds is about as stupid as the next objection ... that it's something you grow out of, like spots on the face.

Now I must admit that about the age of fourteen I gave up going to church. But whatever way you look at it, to give up something at that age is not a rational rejection of it—it wasn't for me. Nobody is mature enough at eleven or fourteen to make up his mind about anything as important as God, Christ and Church. I certainly wasn't ... and a few years later I had second thoughts, like lots of people do, and arrived at what I like to think was a *mature* faith. So I reckon that for anyone to decide at the age of eleven or so, and just on the basis of going to Sunday school for a few years, that Christianity is not for them—well, it just isn't on as an objection, is it?

I suppose having gone to Sunday school is both an advantage and a disadvantage—rather depending on the Sunday school. For me, it meant that I have never been an atheist—I didn't have any problems getting over that first hurdle of belief in God. But for many people Sunday school has given them a completely wrong picture of Christ—I meet people with extraordinary ideas that you can trace back to Sunday school days: coloured pictures of a bearded Jesus who they think is God, songs about heaven above the 'bright blue sky', and generally infantile notions of angels and so on, that they store away in their minds and bring out every now and then as 'evidence' that Christianity is obviously untrue. I know lots of modern Sunday schools aren't a bit like that, but some still are, and they do a great deal of harm. They encourage the idea that Christianity is strictly for kids.

For women and children only?

Which brings us very neatly to the next objection, that only old ladies and young children believe in the Christian faith any longer.

I honestly don't see how anybody can say that when you think of the history of Christianity—you know, being fed to lions and all that. Even today, when I agree there aren't the same physical dangers in being a Christian—not in most countries, at any rate—the problems are just as great, and it still demands a lot of courage and determination to be a Christian. Of course, old ladies can be as brave as anybody else, but I assume the objector feels that somehow Christianity is effeminate or undemanding, when really it requires great moral courage and determination.

But this idea—that men and young people are somehow 'above' believing—has really got around. I think it largely accounts for the fact that in many churches women outnumber men by two or three to one, and in some others there aren't many people at all under, say, thirty. Actually, in my own church this isn't true. Our evening congregation on a Sunday is about seventy-five per cent. under thirty, with nearly as many males as females—but that isn't quite typical all round.

Too many men haven't really looked into Christianity. If they had, they would never reckon it was a soft option—it's not a cake-walk; you have to be on your toes all the time. Incidentally, I think some at least of the people who say it's for women and kids are really using that as an excuse—they know it's demanding and hard, and don't want to get drawn into it. In other words, it can be a coward's excuse.

I ought to add that there seems to be something of a 'revival' of interest in Christianity among young people. I must say wherever I go there seem to be vast numbers of youngsters who are full of questions and eager to find out, not at all prejudiced against the Bible or Christ (but sometimes hung up on the church and that side of things). After all, tens of thousands of people under twenty-five belong to the different Christian youth organisations, and nearly all of these groups are stronger now than they were fifteen or twenty years ago. If Christianity 'comes back', I think the return will be led by the new generation, mini-skirts, pink shirts, chelsea boots and all.

Some young people, of course, hold back from Christianity because they think it will take the fun out of life. They see dark churches, dingy halls and big Bibles, or they meet some fanatical Bible-punchers who fix them with little gimlet eyes and ram texts down their throats, and think that if they are converted to Christ this would have to be their scene.

But they're wrong! There are Christians, of course, who cut themselves off from the rest of the world, and act as though anything enjoyable must be sinful. But the Bible says God gave us everything in the world to be richly enjoyed[3]; that Jesus gives us "life in all its fullness"[4]. I have found being a Christian has increased my sense of pleasure—I enjoy life more, not less. And, while churches and halls may be dark, well, so are discothèques and cellar coffee bars. It's the people in them that count—and the church is *people*, not buildings. Why not come on in and help us brighten the place up a bit?

But why Christianity?

I must say, at any rate in the show-biz world, the most frequent objection to Christianity isn't any of the ones I've dealt with so far, but a general unwillingness to regard it as any more valid than dozens of other religions and philosophies. People love dabbling in religion, rather than committing themselves to anything, so you find them dragging out any set of beliefs, however cooky, just to avoid the challenge of settling for one that makes moral as well as mental demands. They profess a great fascination for reincarnation, astrology, spiritualism, Buddhism and just about every other religion known or unknown.

Now I've got nothing against some of these religions—honestly I don't know too much about them. But they all rely on the ideas or thoughts of men—

[3] I Timothy 6:17   [4] John 10:10

clever, brilliant, perhaps holy, men, but men all the same. The difference in Christianity is that it depends completely on the person of Jesus Christ, and it stands or falls not on whether we prefer his views to all the others, but on whether he is who he claims to be or not. If we decide that he is the Son of God, then there's no more arguing. One man's ideas have no more authority really than another's. That's why Christians believe in a God who has *spoken*, because we simply must have some more reliable guide to life and what it's all about than the conflicting ideas of human beings.

The danger with lots of these other ideas is that they are great substitutes for the real thing. If we believe in a God, we also believe in a Satan, and I think many of these ideas—especially the psychic ones—are his way of distracting people from a genuine relationship with God.

Some of these things seem harmless enough—astrology, for example. I used to read the predictions in the paper, just for fun. After all, they're too general-ised to take seriously. But since I've been a Christian I've felt I shouldn't bother even reading them for laughs. The Bible tells us not to worry about tomorrow[5]. We should hand it over to God, knowing that whatever comes is His will for us.

[5] Matthew 6:34

Objections to Christianity have to be met and answered, where possible. But I'm not kidding myself that if all the objections were answered everyone would be instantly converted. There's a spiritual barrier inside men's minds that only the Holy Spirit can penetrate, and when he does most of these arguments and quibbles disappear. You can't argue your way to God, but arguing (at least, if we're prepared to have an open mind) can at least set us off on a journey towards Him.

No business like show-business

Whom do you admire, professionally? Whom do you most enjoy working with? What were your favourite records? What are your big ambitions for the future? What happened to the Shadows? Have the Settlers taken their place? What do you think about the Eurovision Song Contest? Do you like acting more than singing? How about films—and TV? When did you start writing songs? Which are your favourite countries for working in?

I suppose whatever your line of business, you look up to the people who are one or two steps above you. For myself, I've always admired people who do very well things that I—as yet—can hardly do at all. Just now, for instance, I'm a great admirer of great actors— Sir John Gielgud on stage was an absolute revelation to me. I like Marlon Brando, and Paul Newman, on the screen; and I've always admired Jean Simmons. I thought she was tremendous in *Elmer Gantry*—and I'd better immediately add Burt Lancaster, too.

I haven't worked with any of those people. Of those I have, I particularly enjoyed working with Dora Bryan, Una Stubbs (she's one of those I've got a soft spot for) and Robert Morley.

Funnily enough, before working with Robert Morley in *The Young Ones* I'd been told he was very difficult to work with, so I was a bit apprehensive. But I found him the most charming bloke, and very help- ful. He obviously realised it was my first big part in a film so several times when I went wrong, to cover up for me, he'd make a mistake immediately afterwards and say something like, "Oh I'm so sorry, you'll have to excuse me. I've gone wrong again, do forgive me." I reckoned that was very generous, and nobody else has ever done that for me.

Of course, I've enjoyed working with the Shadows over the years—and all over the world, too. You get to know people pretty well when you're on tour and working night after night together. It's quite a test of personality, believe me!

Favourite Records

I think of all the fifty or so singles I've released, my favourite one was 'The Day I Met Marie', which Hank Marvin wrote and I released in 1967. If anything deserved to reach number one, that was it. In fact, it just made the Top Ten. But 'Congratulations', which —to be honest—I didn't rate too highly, was a massive hit. There's no accounting for taste!

I haven't actually disliked any of my records, remarkable as that may seem. But I think standards have improved since the Shads and I began eleven years ago. If we had faced today's standards we would probably have failed. In those days it was all rock 'n roll, which was exciting but musically and technically simple. Pop has become much more clever and sophisticated, and the public have become more demanding. It's all much more progressive, which means that records now require more thought, better arrangements and more originality. Some of my early hits would sound very simple and corny now.

Future Ambitions

It won't be easy, and it may seem a bit big-headed, but my main ambition now is to be known as an actor as well as a singer. When I did my first really 'straight' piece of acting, in the film *Two a Penny*, people said to me, "Does this mean you're going to give up singing?"

Well, I certainly don't intend to give up singing, so I realise the difficulties involved. Hardly anybody has been really successful in both fields at once. Without

T–C

actually stopping singing—and doing all those happy-go-lucky pop TV shows and so on—it's hard to get serious acting work. Ideally I should go off and do a year or two in rep. somewhere, but that would end my singing career, of course. Still, my ambition is to be an actor one day—I'm quite clear on that.

I've enjoyed the acting I've done so far. *Two a Penny* was the most important thing, but the ITV play I did (which wasn't too brilliant) and the Tyne Tees *Life with Johnny* series have given me valuable experience and I've learnt quite a bit about technique. But so far I've not had a part that stretched me out fully, and so now I'm looking for a part that will do that. I don't mean the parts I've had have been easy—far from it. But they've been limited character-wise, and so haven't demanded much in the way of *range* of acting.

As for minor ambitions, I'd like to do some more cabaret. I enjoy performing at the Talk of the Town, for instance. I'm hoping, too, for some new television ideas, because it's a great medium for a performer.

The Shads and the Setts

I think it's a minor tragedy that the Shadows have broken up. I feel they're the only group with any presentation—and that's bar none. I've yet to see a group on television or on stage present themselves as they did. Maybe towards the end the sound was a bit old, but we're in a visual business as well, and nobody equalled them there.

I think their break-up was quite unnecessary. They had done very well in Britain and all over the world for some time without having hit records, and there was still a great demand for them. However, each of them was getting ambitious in his own way. Hank has gone solo. Bruce Welch is working in music publishing. Brian Bennett is involved in music production, and John Rostill is free-lancing and composing. Probably they will get together sometimes for a 'special', but I think they've finished with regular touring for good. In a way I can understand their feelings after ten years of touring and having no individual freedom. It's much more difficult for a group than for a solo artist.

Of course, as far as I'm concerned there's nothing new about working apart from the Shadows. For three years I've been recording and performing without them. When we made the 'Established 1958' LP (in 1968) it was the first time we'd been together in a recording studio for over a year. It wasn't a sudden break at all.

I started working with the Settlers in Gospel concerts in the Spring of 1968, so I suppose it's not surprising that people began to think of them as the Shads' successors. In fact, as I've already said, I had virtually stopped working with a group some time before that, and I doubt if I shall ever have another 'backing group' as such. In any case, the Settlers are not and have never been a 'backing' group. We've worked together on Gospel concerts, on seven or eight television shows of a religious nature, and may well do more work together in the future, including perhaps some records. But they are a distinctive group, with their own career to make, and neither of us want people to think of us as permanently linked.

I first saw the Settlers in a concert at the Royal Festival Hall. Cindy Kent—their girl singer—had just joined our church, and a group of us went along to see the show. I must admit I was quite knocked out with it. About that time I'd been invited to do some Gospel concerts on the Continent, and badly needed a suitable group to accompany me.

The Settlers aren't a 'Gospel' group—they're a very good all-round sort of cabaret act in the general folk-pop style—but they'd got quite a number of Gospel songs in their repertoire. We asked them if they'd be interested in coming on the tour, they agreed—and the concerts went down a bomb. In fact, the reception by the audience in Zagreb, Yugoslavia, was the most fantastic thing in all my career. They were still sitting in their seats cheering and clapping as we were being driven away from the theatre!

Some people are a bit surprised that I can fit in with a basically folky group like the Settlers. In fact, I've always done quite a few country and western style songs, and the Setts have always veered towards pop, so really we're a happy compromise.

That Eurovision thing

I enjoyed representing Britain in the Eurovision Song Contest, even though I didn't win. After all, it gave me one of my biggest hit records and a gold disc for over a million sales. I suppose it's possible to take it all too seriously, and I think the voting is right up the spout!

Personally, I think the only way to make any sense of the competition is to make it a bit more complicated. At the moment it is very obvious that the national votes do not represent the popular tastes of that country. 'Congratulations' outsold the Spanish winning entry 'La la la' in every competing country—including Spain! It's probably been the same with Lulu's song in 1969. So we want a method that will truly reflect popular opinion.

So why not do on a European scale what we do here in Britain to choose our entry? Each national singer could sing his or her entry twice on one Saturday evening, on the Eurovision network. Then viewers all over Europe could be invited to send their votes to their national TV station—excluding their own country's entry, of course. Then the following week another hook-up could produce the votes from each country—not, I should have thought, the total of votes cast for each song, but simply that country's vote cast for whichever of the songs had been proved to be the most popular with the viewers in that country ... one vote from each country. So far as I can see, in that way you would have a very good chance of discovering the song in the competition which is genuinely the most *popular*, and all the two hundred million viewers, or however many it is, would feel that they had had some say in its choice. At the moment it's pretty obvious that many of the juries do not represent the tastes of their own country.

Now so far as I'm personally concerned, I've got no complaints. Far from feeling peeved that 'Congratulations' didn't win the Contest, I must say it was probably the best thing, professionally, that has ever happened to me. Wherever I went for the next couple of years I got this instant sympathy from audiences—all over Europe!—and everyone would say "Of course, it should have won." To make their point, they went out and bought the record—and it sold over a million copies. So ... I should worry! But I still feel we should have the fairest and most representative way of arriving at the results in a competition with such enormous prestige, and financial rewards, as this one. The temptation to let national or commercial interests sway the juries' voting is just too great under the present system.

Some people thought—and told me—that I was putting my career in jeopardy by agreeing to represent Britain in the Eurovision Song Contest. Their idea was that I was on a hiding to nothing. If I won—well, what do you expect of such an established recording artist? If I lost—see, Cliff Richard's finished, beaten by some unheard-of singer from Gothenburg or somewhere.

But I had already managed to convince myself that this was a contest between *songs*, not singers. In any case, any artist who has been recording for a few years has the occasional mediocre hit or near-miss. You just have to accept them and take them in your stride. At worst (I argued) the Eurovision British entry would be the equivalent of a mediocre hit, and seeing that the public vote for our national entry it must, quite apart from quality, have some popular appeal. In fact, of course, it was a smash hit, and losing the Contest, as I say, turned out to be the best thing I could have done.

Incidentally, I thought the 1969 Contest was an absolute farce, with four songs tied for first place—

'everybody shall win, and everybody shall have prizes'. I reckon this makes the whole thing look ridiculous, and I hope the organisers make sure that it never happens again. Perhaps they could have a 'sing-off'!

It's Dangerous to have Favourites

I'm often asked which are my favourite overseas countries for working in. That's a bit of a trap question, and I like to know which country the person is from before I answer it! In fact, I've always had a pretty good reception in every country I've worked in. Pop fans are much the same the world over.

But obviously some places stand out. As I've already mentioned, Yugoslavia in 1968 was fantastic —up to now the most tremendous reception and response I've ever seen. In fact, when we arrived at the airport in Zagreb there was this huge banner hanging from the main buildings—CLIFF AND THE SETTLERS WELCOME TO ZAGREB. And from then on they just overwhelmed us! I think it was the first Gospel song concert they'd ever had in the country, and they certainly made the most of it.

Other than Yugoslavia, Rumania and Paris stand out in my mind. There must be something about Eastern Europe! I went to Rumania for the first time early in 1969, and the welcome and audience reaction was terrific. Perhaps the main difference between these audiences and British or, say, German, ones is that they listen, in complete silence, to the songs—no screams or shouts—and then burst into prolonged applause when they have ended. Fans in countries where records are endlessly played and plugged don't seem to be very bothered whether they actually hear the song or not. The audiences in Paris are also different from the usual run of West European ones. They listen, too, in silence, and save their appreciation for the end of the song. We've had some fantastic audiences in Paris, over the years. For me, this is perfection in audiences—silence throughout the numbers, and then thunderous applause afterwards. Most of us would like to take audiences like that on tour with us!

Germany, Sweden and Holland, where there are a lot of fans, are much more like Britain—great fun, and plenty of enthusiasm: perhaps a bit too much, sometimes. Judging by memories of a few years ago, the same thing applies to Australia and New Zealand. Japan is quite different—no four minute standing ovations there! You do your number, there's this great roar, lasting about five seconds, and then it dies away instantly and they're sitting there silently, waiting for the next number. They don't like it if you take too long introducing it, either! I remember that African audiences—especially in South Africa—were like this, too.

Racialism

Mentioning South Africa introduces the subject of race and racialism. It's many years since I was in South Africa, and I must say at that time—before apartheid and so on were such hot topics in Britain—I hadn't thought much about it. When I got back to Britain someone asked me what I felt about the 'troubles' in South Africa, and I replied, "What troubles?" The truth is I hadn't seen any and didn't know much about it. From that, some people arrived at the conclusion that I didn't care about the problems of non-Whites in South Africa. That wasn't so, but I don't see any point in making statements about subjects I know very little about.

Now I would want to be more definite. As I see it, the Bible is quite clear about this: racialism of any kind, in any place, is *out*. No one race, or skin-colour, is better than another in God's sight. He doesn't have any favourites.

What people forget is that this cuts two ways. There are prejudiced black people as well as prejudiced white ones—I was shocked to hear what some of the

Black Muslims believe. The simple ideal is that every individual has equal rights, as a human being. It's then up to him to learn to live with his neighbour, whether he's black, yellow or white. We've learnt, over a long period, to put up with our white neighbours, even when we dislike them. Racial prejudice, though, makes us put up barriers towards a black neighbour before we've really got to know him as a man.

In this matter, perhaps ordinary people can learn something from the show-biz world, because there the only criterion is talent and the colour of a person's skin just doesn't come into it. There's probably no 'trade' so well integrated racially as the entertainment business. Perhaps that, at least, can be put down to its credit!

Whatever happened to Two a Penny?

I often get asked what 'happened' to *Two a Penny*. We made this film in 1967, shooting it on location in London, and it had a run at a West End cinema in the Summer of 1968. Since that run, it has become obvious that the big circuits are rather afraid of it, and many people have been disappointed that it hasn't been shown in their areas.

I must say I'm more than a trifle annoyed about this. It may sound immodest, but I reckon it's quite a good film, certainly every bit as good as the average ones that get general release. As something of a film fan I see enough current films to know that some pretty poor stuff gets released. For myself, I think *Two a Penny* is by a long way the best thing I've done on the screen—but the critics seemed completely hung up by its connection with Billy Graham, and wrote it off as crude propaganda. I think this frightened off cinemagoers, and scared the circuits.

But in fact the film is basically entertainment, and those critics who managed to watch the film rather than decide in advance that it was all a big religious con admitted that. The audiences who saw it enjoyed it, whether they accepted the indirect 'message' in it or not. This is proved by the fact that it was voted ninth Best Film of the Year in the *Disc* poll, even though it was only shown for six weeks in London during 1968.

I can't understand why distributors aren't prepared to take a risk on this sort of film. It annoys me to find people are only prepared to back certainties. They think that because this film has some Christian content it will do poor business. But *Going my Way* had Christian content. So did *Quo Vadis* and *Ben Hur*. They didn't do too badly.

I'm not suggesting *Two a Penny* is in that class, of course. But all the same, first and foremost it's a *film*, and the message is incidental to the story, coming naturally out of the characters and events. Certainly plenty of Christians felt it went too far that way, and was too secular and indefinite in its message. So you see, you can't win!

How about Writing

One of the things I'd like to do more of is writing songs. In the past I've been credited with a share in some of my own hits (I still get royalties for my part in writing 'Bachelor Boy'!), but in the last couple of years I've got quite keen on the idea, and you can often find me surrounded by mikes, amplifiers and tapes trying out ideas for new songs in my home.

One reason for this was an urgent need to find some new 'Gospel' material. I started off with a repertoire of about three Gospel songs, but with—often—two or three Christian meetings a week this soon began to look and sound a bit thin. On digging around, I found that really there wasn't very much available in my kind of style, and what there was either had ghastly words (and they say pop songs are corny!) or instantly forgettable tunes.

As a result, I put a couple of new tunes to some good sets of words I came across. One song was by Valerie Hadert, who spends most of her life in hospital. That was called 'Think Again'. The other was by Keith Craddock, and was the winning 'words' entry in a competition to 'write a song for Cliff' organised by *Crusade* magazine. It's called 'Reflections', and it has made a great hit, especially in college and school meetings.

Then I collaborated with director Jim Collier to write the three new songs in *Two a Penny*—one of them, 'Questions', is printed at the front of this book. After that, the *Life with Johnny* television series really got me involved in writing in a way I have never been before. We—David Winter, the Settlers and I—wrote no less than twenty brand new songs for the series. In most cases David wrote the lyrics and either Mike Jones or I produced a melody. But just to keep the males in their places, Cindy produced a couple of really lovely tunes, one of them ('Love is More than Words') perhaps the most melodious of them all—and we all shared in the basic ideas, treatments, harmonies and so on. It's a very fascinating experience to hear a song you first picked out one chord at a time on an acoustic guitar performed with full arrangement, musicians and voices!

Life with Johnny was, in fact, great fun. Our only disappointment was that, for some reason we've never really discovered, the series was not fully networked. Basically, the shows were Bible stories (parables, sayings of Christ and so on) presented in an up to date way, in a modern setting, and with new songs, drama and dance. It was quite ambitious, and I think it's all credit to Tyne Tees for having the courage to try something completely new and different in 'religious' programmes.

To me that's the main attraction in my work now—doing new and different things. My big battle is to avoid being labelled and kept in a certain narrow field of entertainment. I still get film scripts sent to me with red buses in, but I don't want all my films to be just Cliff Richard extravaganzas. I don't particularly want the big billing. I'm looking for new ideas, things that will present me with a challenge and keep me from getting stale or stereotyped.

People matter more than things

Do you need other people? Could you get by without friends? Would you say you were a good mixer? Do you have any girl friends? What would be your ideal evening out? Weekend? Holiday? What puts you off people most? What do you think about fans and fanaticism?

Friendship is very important to me. A few people—very few—like to be hermits and live on their own, but surely it's a basic need that people should have other people around them. Of course, we like to get away at times and be on our own, but even then it often means meeting people. Yes, to me it's very important to have friends—close friends—and I've been fortunate enough all my life to have good friends. We had a close, friendly family, too, and it's only in recent years that, through circumstances mainly, we've tended to drift apart a bit.

I don't often see any of my old school-friends—just two or three, and that I put down to my career. Not that I pulled away from them, but when I got well

known many of my old friends, and even some of my
relatives, seemed to get shy and not want to keep up
friendship.

Nowadays pretty well all of my close friends are not
in show-biz. I think that's a tremendous advantage.
It was more difficult when I was always on tour or
working, and could never really get to know anybody
outside the business. But now I value tremendously
this 'other life', to off-set the rather fake world of
show-biz, and depend a lot on my friends to balance
things up. I'm not saying I don't have any friends in
show-biz, but they are friends not because they're in
the business but because they're who they are. Their
work doesn't matter. Even if I went back to touring
and so on, I know now that I should insist on making
time for doing other things as well.

Being a good mixer

I suppose I've never been shy, and I've always enjoyed good company, but I don't think I'm too well
qualified to tell people how to be good mixers. I'm
sure one secret is to be a good listener, and I must
admit that isn't naturally one of my strong points.
Still, I'm working at it, and developing a good, strong,
yes-I'm-very-interested-in-what-you're-saying   look
for boring conversationalists. A good mixer stimulates

the flow of conversation but doesn't dominate—which is just my problem! Still, genuinely to like people is half the battle, and I think I make out all right there.

Girl friends

At the time of writing, I don't have a 'girl friend' in the recognised sense of the words, but among my circle of friends there are a few girls, of course. But unless you marry her, I don't see how you can have a really close friendship with a girl. I'm sure that if I got engaged, then that 'friendship' would dominate all others; but short of that it is obviously very difficult to have the sort of relationship with a girl which a man has with a close male friend.

Let me explain. Some people talk about 'platonic' friendships, by which I think they mean a man and woman having a friendship comparable to that between two men or two women, and free of any sexual complications. Personally I doubt if that is possible, or at any rate very difficult. It could even be dangerous or misleading.

Still, there are girls I admire and have a soft spot for, and I certainly count them among my friends.

Ideal relaxation?

For me, any ideal evening out would have to include a meal! A theatre date—or perhaps even better, a new film—and then off somewhere for a long, lingering meal, unspoilt by any thought of having to get up early the next morning. That doesn't happen very often, but when it does it's just about my favourite way of relaxing with friends. Sometimes after working, too—a long day on set or in the studio—a relaxed meal, with good conversation and no sense of hurry, makes a super end to the day. I'm glad to see that's a pleasure that our Lord enjoyed, too.

Weekends are more difficult for me, because a 'weekend' often gets reduced to one day. Again, it's that feeling of relaxation that makes a good weekend. Going away, especially in the Summer, can help, but sitting around doing things as the fancy takes you, having tea in the garden, and that sort of thing, makes for an ideal rest. In any case, I make it a rule—broken only in the direst emergency—never to work on Sundays, so even if my weekend is reduced to just one day I do get that essential time for rest, as well as for Christian worship and service.

So far as holidays are concerned, my tastes are very simple. I like sun and water. Provided the weather's good—and that's a big proviso—I'd be as happy cruising in my boat on the Broads as anywhere more exotic. Some of my best holidays have been helping to lead Broads cruises for the boys in our Crusader Bible class. During the day we enjoy the outdoor life, canoeing and that sort of thing, and then in the evenings we gather in one of the cabins for talk, discussion and argument about some aspect of Christianity.

You can go off people, you know

You can get 'put off' people at your first meeting with them, which somehow seems a bit unfair. Sometimes when you get to know them better you find your first impressions were quite wrong.

Generally speaking, loud-mouthed people put me off most of all—the sort you can hear halfway across a restaurant filling everyone else in on their views about life, the neighbours and so on.

Close behind them come people who try to monopolise you. People in the public eye suffer from this, and I've had my share. These people seem to think that because you're 'famous' they own you, and you must instantly drop everything else to give them your attention. Sometimes—just twice, I think—people have really annoyed me by trying to twist my arm to do things (even for good causes) or by demanding my time or company. Normally, if I'm asked to do something, I'll try my best to help, but these people force the issue. I can be very stubborn in those circumstances!

I'm glad to say it has practically never happened in my 'private' life. The strange thing is, the closer my friends are, the less they try to twist my arm!

I've suffered a bit, too, in the past from what a friend of mine calls 'forward women'. Again, this is an occupational hazard for performers. I say "in the past", because I've learnt to spot them a mile off and take evasive action. If they knew how much it put me off, they'd probably stop trying it on.

The worst sort of fans put me off, too—the sort who think they own you. I must say many of my fans —the vast majority—have been very decent and they haven't made a nuisance of themselves. But there's a small minority who are a bit of a pest. Some try to dog your foot-steps wherever you go. Obviously no-one objects to a bit of admiration, but there is a danger when fans get too involved emotionally. The whole thing can get out of balance then.

Some of the best fans in Britain are up in the North-East—Geordie-land. They are very polite and not at all aggressive. Then there are what I call 'regulars'—they don't 'dog' me but simply support me wherever I'm appearing. I just wish a few of the more strident ones in other places would take a lesson or two from them!

Still, I'm not complaining. Considering how many people I meet, week in and week out, very few 'put me off'. I've got plenty of good friends I can rely on, and a manager and a recording manager who I count as long-standing personal friends. Through Christianity, too, I count myself a 'brother' to countless people all round the world, most of whom I have never met, who share the same Father and serve the same Master.

Will someone please explain . . .

*The Trinity . . . How prayer works . . . The Holy Spirit
. . . How sin can be forgiven?*

Because of my own problems with the subject during
the long period when I was searching and asking
questions about Christianity, I have great sympathy
with those who find the idea of the Trinity (God as
Father, Son and Holy Spirit) rather baffling.

I sometimes think that many of these problems are
connected with terminology, and that Christians
could make it a lot easier—or at least much less confusing—if they were a bit more precise and careful in
the way they speak of God and Christ. When we talk
about 'Three-in-One and One-in-Three', or loosely
call Jesus 'God', without differentiating between the
different 'members' of the Trinity, then the difficulties
are strictly of terminology.

When you really sit down and thrash this subject
out, though, you find that many of these loose phrases
and descriptions are just confusing the issue. If we call

Jesus 'God', without explaining what we mean, then obviously anyone who thinks about it is going to ask who was running heaven when Jesus Christ was on earth. In fact, of course, the heavens weren't evacuated when he was a man. God the Father continued to rule the Universe, and Jesus often spoke to him in prayer and told others to do the same.

So clearly there is a difference between the three Persons who make up the Trinity, but their nature is one and they are each equally divine.

So I think it's fairly important to distinguish between God the Father, God the Son (Jesus Christ) and God the Holy Spirit. For instance, we usually pray, guided *by* the Spirit within us, *to* the Father *through* the Son. Obviously it is possible to pray to Christ, and presumably to the Holy Spirit. Certainly Christ on earth accepted worship. But it helps most people to get the pattern of Persons right. It certainly helps me!

I remember something Shelley Berman, a Jew, said on David Frost's TV programme. Frost kept talking about 'God', until Berman interrupted.

"Look here," he said, "His name's Jehovah. God's his occupation."

That's really quite helpful. God is his 'occupation' —or, more precisely, his nature. And the Father shares that nature with two other Persons, Jesus Christ and the Holy Spirit. Three Persons, but one

God: it's not really quite so complicated as we sometimes think, or as we Christians carelessly make it.

I must say, the Holy Spirit is a subject I know little about, beyond that I believe He is the power behind anything I do that is worth doing. Perhaps that is part of His character—to be the silent, invisible member of the Trinity, working away in the world and in the lives of Christians, achieving the will of God.

What about prayer?

I have always prayed, but since becoming a Christian I think my prayers have become less selfish. Perhaps that's why I'm much more aware nowadays of their being answered.

The strange thing is that, as a Christian, I believe God hears and answers prayer, but I'm still knocked out and quite overcome when He actually does it! I think of prayer as the way God gets us in on His activity in the world and in people's lives. To me, it's a great privilege. It's as though we are given the chance to share in God's work.

I usually try to divide my prayers up into thanks and worship, confession and prayer for others. It's very easy to slip into just going through a great long list of requests to God, without even pausing to remind ourselves who He is, or how unworthy we really are to come to Him. In prayer for others I include relatives and friends, people I've got a particular responsibility for, and those who for one reason or another are on my mind or in my thoughts.

Personally I've never even tried to get on terms with the use of 'thee' and 'thou'. Fortunately, when I became a Christian the people I most often prayed with were ones who talked simply and naturally to God, in ordinary, everyday language. I feel sorry for young Christians who try to express sincere and important prayers in a language that died out hundreds of years ago. I think many hold back from praying aloud with others for fear that they can't express themselves 'properly'. This is really a tragedy. It's what we say to God, not how we say it, that matters.

Understanding the Cross

Obviously the cross is important to Christians. It's the most common Christian symbol, and you see people wearing crosses, crosses on graves and in churches, and so on. But it's much more than simply a badge of Christianity, and it would be a pity if anyone were to get the idea that that is all it is.

Christianity, like many religions, is based on the idea that between God, who is good and holy, and men, who are not, there is a vast gulf. This has come about through man breaking God's laws and falling short of his standards. Christians believe that the cross is God's way of bridging the gap.

Can I put it like this. The thing that comes between us and God is our sin. There are no barriers on His side—they're all on ours: or, rather, are made by us. The problem of mankind is how to get rid of our sin, and so remove the barrier between us and God.

That is what Jesus Christ came into the world to do. He lived a life without any sin at all. So when He died —or rather, was put to death—on the cross on the first Good Friday, He couldn't have been dying for his own sins: He had never committed any.

In fact, He was dying for *our* sins: yours and mine.

And now, if we turn to Him, truly sorry for our past sin and wanting to be rid of it, God forgives us because Jesus Christ has died for it.

> *There was no other good enough*
> *To pay the price of sin;*
> *He only could unlock the gate*
> *Of heaven and let us in.*

The old children's hymn about the cross puts it very neatly.

Now that's all right for sin in the past, before I became a Christian. But what about sin now? Can that be forgiven as well?

Yes, it can. "If we confess our sins, he is faithful and just to forgive us our sins." That's what St. John says.

But wouldn't that encourage Christians just to go on sinning, in the belief that God will go on forgiving them for Christ's sake?

You might think it would. But in fact it doesn't work out like that at all. To be truly sorry for sin ('repentance' is the proper word) includes a real determination not to commit the sin again. Often, of course, we shall fail—over and over again. But each time we turn to God for forgiveness we must honestly regret having failed and sincerely want to be done with it. God reads our hearts, and he knows what our true desire is, whatever we may say with our lips. He knows if there is a real longing in our hearts to be free from sin.

I think it was Luther who said, "The truest repentance is to do it no more." If that's right, then the next best repentance is not to *want* to do it any more. It's the inner attitude that counts.

No Christian who has been through it would feel that real repentance—seeing what our sins did to Jesus Christ—is an easy option or a licence to go on sinning.

But when we do 'repent' God keeps his word, and forgives us completely. There is no need for us to bear the weight one moment longer of sins God is willing and able to forgive, if we would only turn to Him. One of the greatest things about the Christian faith is this possibility of forgiveness. There are few of us who aren't conscious that we need to be forgiven, and in Jesus Christ God has made it possible for everyone who repents and trusts in Christ to have that need met ... and not just on one big, important occasion when the past is cleared, but day by day too, as we bring to Him all the comparatively small but yet important things that trouble our consciences.

One last word

I hope you've enjoyed reading this book, and feel it's answered some of the questions you would like to have asked me if you'd had the chance. At the same time, I hope it's set you asking yourself a few questions.

This last, short chapter is really just some final, random thoughts about life that don't quite fit under the other headings.

For instance, does my conscience bother me about being rich? Some people say I can afford to be holy . . . it's the sort of luxury they can't afford.

To me that's ludicrous. Being a Christian has nothing at all to do with being rich. Actually, according to Jesus, it's far harder being a Christian if you're rich[1] than if you're poor.

You see, having money is a responsibility for a Christian. He's expected to keep his accounts for it with God as well as his accountant. In the Bible there were good rich men, and bad ones. It wasn't the amount of money that made the difference, but what

[1] Luke 18:24–27

they did with it. Nobody knows what I do with my money (except God), so I don't see how anybody can say what effect it has on my Christianity, or the way I live.

I can say this, though. None of the things that really matter to me depends on money, so not having it couldn't deprive me of anything really important.

I never think about the money I earn. To me, that side of things is secondary to the 'artistic' side. I just want to be left alone to sing and try to act. I certainly don't have a crisis of conscience about the money I earn—but I would have if I thought I was wasting it.

It's a bit the same with this business of success. I'd hate to have been a fringe pop star, I must admit, and it's great to think that if everything flopped tomorrow I'd be able to look back on a career with eleven years at somewhere around the top and many wonderful high spots to remember. But what you never have, you never miss. And if that hadn't been the course my life was to take, I still believe God would have planned for me other things that would be just as satisfying and fulfilling, provided I put Him first.

In the same way, I don't know what lies in the future for me. Nobody does. But I believe the Bible means what it says: "All things work together for good for those who love God." I'm prepared to accept that and live my life by it.

I've not stopped asking questions myself—not by a long way. But I think I have found the answer to the most important question of all: what's life *for*? If you haven't got an answer to that, nothing—money, sex, fame—*nothing* will ever make you really happy.

For me, life is for finding and knowing God. That is why Jesus Christ came into the world, and that is the whole object of our existence on earth. Life only begins, really, when we come to know and trust the Person who made us, and who wants to welcome us to Himself.

To me, that makes perfect sense.